ANALYZE THE ANCIENTS

# ANCIENT Rome

Louise Spilsbury

Gareth Stevens PUBLISHING

Please visit our website, www.garethstevens.com.

For a free color catalog of all our high-quality books, call toll free 1-800-542-2595 or fax 1-877-542-2596.

Cataloging-in-Publication Data

Names: Spilsbury, Louise.
Title: Ancient Rome / Louise Spilsbury.
Description: New York : Gareth Stevens Publishing, 2019. | Series: Analyze the ancients | Includes glossary and index.
Identifiers: LCCN ISBN 9781538225592 (pbk.) | ISBN 9781538225585 (library bound)
Subjects: LCSH: Rome--Civilization--Juvenile literature.
Classification: LCC DG77.S646 2019 | DDC 937'.06--dc23

First Edition

Published in 2019 by
Gareth Stevens Publishing
111 East 14th Street, Suite 349
New York, NY 10003



Produced for Gareth Stevens by Calcium Creative Ltd
Editors: Sarah Eason and Jennifer Sanderson
Designers: Paul Myerscough and Jessica Moon
Picture researcher: Rachel Blount

Picture credits: Cover: Shutterstock: Sabrina Marchi; Inside: Shutterstock: Fernando Cortes: p. 41; Cpaulfell: p. 32; Maurizio De Mattei: p. 8; Evannovostro: p. 5; Yory Frenklakh: pp. 11, 45; Sandor Gora: p. 22; Javarman: p. 35; Joeborg: p. 31; Ruslan Kalnitsky: p. 43; Kiev.Victor: p. 7; Luxerendering: p. 16; Marcovarro: p. 23; Brian Maudsley: p. 6; Mountainpix: p. 37; Nakarin: p. 40; Regien Paassen: p. 15; Radoslaw: p. 4; Valery Rokhin: p. 19; StevanZZ: p. 28; Repina Valeriya: p. 30; Xseon: p. 12; Bukhta Yurii: p. 27; Zuktenvos: p. 10; Wikimedia Commons: pp. 1, 36; Jean-Christophe BENOIST: p. 29; Caliga10's wife: p. 13; Daderot: pp. 20, 42; Jérémy-Günther-Heinz Jähnic: p. 14; Ad Meskens: p. 38; Adrian Pingstone: p. 33; Carole Raddato: pp. 9, 26; Sailko: pp. 17, 24, 34; Wolfgang Sauber: p. 21; Shako: p. 25; Wellcome Images: p. 18; Greg Willis: p. 39.



Printed in the United States of America

CPSIA compliance information: Batch #CS18GS: For further information, contact Gareth Stevens, New York, New York at 1-800-542-2595.

# CONTENTS

# CHAPTER 1

# The Rise of Rome

Around 2,000 years ago, the city of Rome was at the center of a huge **empire** that stretched from England to Africa and from Syria to Spain. The Romans spread their **culture**, their way of life, and their Latin language far and wide. At the peak of its power, Rome ruled more than 45 million people, which means one-quarter of the world's people lived under Roman rule.

## The Legend of Rome

The Romans had a famous **legend** that tells how twin brothers Romulus and Remus founded the city of Rome. The boys were the sons of the god Mars and an evil uncle left them to drown in the Tiber River. They were rescued and raised by a female wolf. When the boys grew up, they killed their uncle and set out to start a new city together. However, they could not agree on where to build the city or what to call it. They had a terrible fight and Remus was killed, leaving Romulus to start a new city. He named the new city "Roma" after himself.

ROMULUS AND REMUS

**This is a statue of the she-wolf feeding the twin boys Romulus and Remus. This became a famous symbol of the founding of the city of Rome and the start of the Roman Empire.**

# The First Emperor of Rome

Rome began as a small town on the banks of the Tiber River. It grew and prospered through trade because its position on the river made it easy for **merchants** to transport goods. Early Rome was ruled by kings, until 509 BC, when the city's people drove out the last king. Rome became a **republic**. The people voted in a group of men called senators, who shared power and governed the state. During the 450 years of the republic, Rome conquered the rest of Italy, then expanded into France, Spain, Turkey, North Africa, and Greece. As Rome grew more powerful, so did its army and its generals. In 49 BC, a powerful general named Julius Caesar wanted to rule the city like a king again. Although Caesar was killed in 43 BC, the mood in Rome had changed. A few years later, Caesar's nephew and **heir**, Octavius, took power. In 27 BC, Octavius became the first **emperor** of Rome.

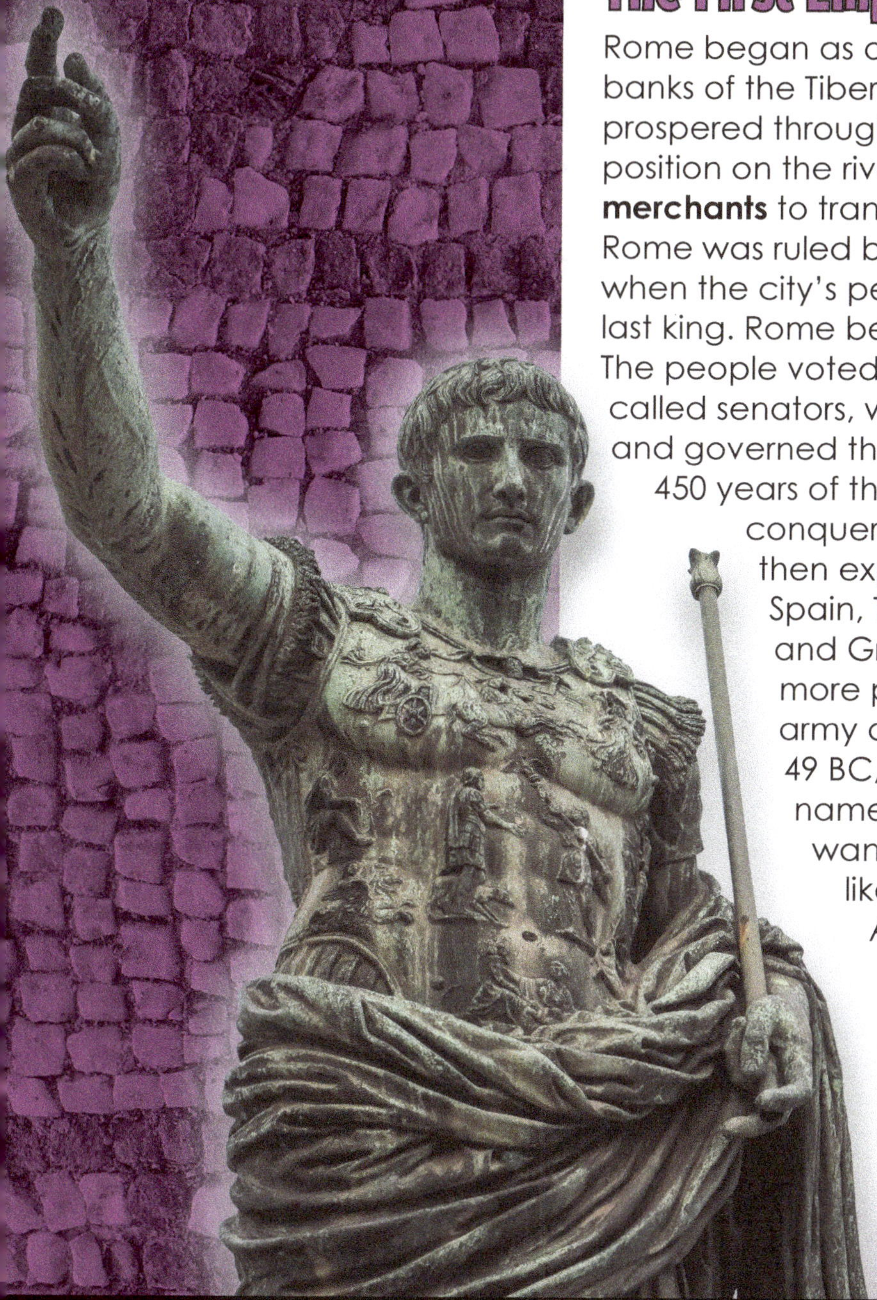

A NOBLE EMPEROR

**This is a statue of Octavius, the first emperor of Rome. He was known as Emperor Caesar Augustus, the name Augustus meaning "superior" or "noble."**

# The Roman Empire

The Roman emperors decided who should rule the land and gave jobs to people they trusted. Gradually, later emperors and their armies expanded their power. Rome's army was the most powerful in the world. It helped create the enormous Roman Empire by conquering even more people and gaining more land.

## Why Rome Expanded

Rome's earliest conquests were mainly against tribes, or groups of people, from cities nearby who attacked Rome. Roman soldiers then fought back and conquered them. To prevent enemies attacking again, some Romans settled among them and introduced the Roman ways of life to the conquered peoples. With more settlements farther away from Rome, the empire expanded to protect these new regions. As Rome became successful and expanded, it needed more land to provide for all its people. Other reasons for building the empire were fame and glory. When leaders, generals, or soldiers won a great battle, they won fame. They also received land and a share of the treasures taken in war.

### ROMAN ROADS

**The Roman army built long, very straight roads so that troops could move from one place to another as quickly and efficiently as possible.**

THE ROMAN FORUM

The Roman Forum was a central area of Rome that had temples, bustling public spaces, and several important government buildings from which the Roman Empire was controlled.

## A Roman Way of Life

As well as conquering peoples, the army helped expand the Roman Empire by building forts and roads to keep Roman areas safe from attacks. The Romans used rivers or mountains as boundaries, or built boundary walls to mark out their empire. They created **provinces** inside the boundaries. In the provinces, the Romans established a Roman way of life and built **temples** to Roman gods and goddesses. They encouraged newly conquered people to live like Romans. Some local **customs** survived in some areas, but most people in the Roman Empire followed Roman rules. They also built the same styles of buildings and used the same objects that other people did all over the Roman world.

# Examining Evidence

There are many different kinds of evidence that hold clues to the lives of the Romans. Archaeologists are people who study ancient cultures. They use the evidence they find to piece together the mysteries of the past.

## History Detectives

The Romans left behind a lot of written evidence in the form of histories, stories, and official documents, such as government and army records. Inscriptions are words carved in stone, metal, wood, or other materials. They tell us names of important people, about Roman gods and goddesses, and record great military victories. Archaeologists can study remains of buildings, some of which are buried underground. They can also study **artifacts** that the Romans made, used, and threw away or buried with their dead, such as clothes, pots, tools, jewelry, and coins. Animal bones found by archaeologists are often remains of people's dinners and can tell us what meat they ate.

RUINS THAT TELL STORIES

**This basilica (church) is in Volubilis, near Meknes in Morocco. Ruins of basilicas, a marketplace, and buildings used by government officials as law courts tell us that the Roman Empire once ruled the area.**

## Pompeii

One of the most amazing records of Roman life is the ruins of the town of Pompeii in Italy. In AD 79, Pompeii was buried under ash and rock when the nearby volcano Mount Vesuvius suddenly erupted. The city lay buried and perfectly preserved for 1,600 years until its discovery. Its treasures show how the very rich lived. They also reveal the kinds of houses, stores, and other artifacts used by the ordinary people in the Roman world. For example, some are shown with symbols, such as scrolls and tablets. These show the importance of education and that educated Romans were proud of their knowledge. The way ordinary women are pictured shows that many had to work for a living, but they were valued in society.

### ANALYZE THE ANCIENTS

This fresco (wall painting) of a baker and his wife was found in the ruins of Pompeii. Based on the information you have learned, can you answer these questions to analyze the Romans? Check your conclusions against the Answers section on pages 44–45.

1. The painting shows the husband holding a papyrus (paper) scroll and the wife holding a writing tablet. What does this tell us about the Romans?

2. The wife is shown standing next to and even slightly in front of her husband. What does this suggest about their relationship and the role of women in ancient Rome?

CHAPTER 2

# Wars and Weapons

The Roman army was the most advanced of its time. Its soldiers were well trained, they fought with the most dangerous weapons, and they wore the safest armor. Their armies were so good that when the Romans invaded Britain, they defeated enemies that had forces ten times bigger than theirs.

## Hand Weapons

The Roman soldier's main weapons were a short sword called a gladius and a long spear called a pilum. The gladius was quite small and light, which made it good for stabbing and slashing in **close combat**. The pilum consisted of a thin, flexible pole made from wood with a sharp iron spike at the end. When a soldier threw it at an enemy's shield, the point got stuck in the shield and the pole of the pilum bent. This made it very hard to pull out and made the shield awkward to use, so the enemy would have to throw the shield away. Some soldiers were also skilled at shooting bows and arrows, or using slingshots to fling stones at enemies.

### DAGGERS

**Roman soldiers also carried daggers in their belts that they could grab when they needed an extra weapon.**

### DEADLY DONKEY

**To use a Roman onager, a stone was placed on the top of the beam, which was pulled back tight. When the beam was suddenly released, the stone was thrown a great distance.**

## Mighty Machines

Roman soldiers used larger weapons to attack a fort or a city's defenses. An onager was like a giant, wooden catapult. It could fire large stones or balls of burning tar. The name "onager" means "wild donkey" because the end of the machine often kicked up like a donkey when it was fired. The Romans also used giant **battering rams** to knock down gates. They made a large siege tower on wheels that could be rolled up to the enemy's walls. It had a drawbridge that lowered from the top of it so soldiers inside could shoot enemies at the top with bows and arrows or climb onto the enemy's walls. They also used a kind of large wind-up crossbow called a ballista, which could hurl a 50-pound (23 kg) stone more than 547 yards (500 m).

# Roman Soldiers

The soldiers who made up the Roman army were all men older than the age of 20. Roman soldiers had to swear an oath of obedience and stayed in the army for at least 20 years. Then they were given land or a farm where they could live in their retirement. Many Roman soldiers came not from Rome or even Italy, but from other parts of the empire including Africa, France, Germany, Spain, and the Middle East.

## Life As a Soldier

Roman soldiers were trained to be tough. They marched up to 20 miles (32 km) a day, wearing all their armor and carrying their weapons, shield, food, and camping equipment, such as cooking pots and spades. Roman soldiers wore sandals that were strong and light. They had iron studs in the leather soles to make them last longer, because they had to walk such long distances. Soldiers could be beaten, whipped, or killed as punishment for disobeying orders or for acting cowardly. Salt was so valuable in Roman times that a soldier was partly paid in salt. The Latin word *salarium,* meaning "salt money," describes the allowance of salt that was paid to Roman soldiers. From that word, we get the word "salary," meaning wages.

### HORSE-HAIR PLUMES

**Roman officers' helmets had plumes of horse hair to show their position or rank.**

ROMAN ARMOR

These men are wearing modern reconstructions of the armor Roman soldiers wore to protect them against being wounded.

## A Soldier's Uniform

A soldier's uniform consisted of a layer of armor made from interlocking strips of iron and leather. These were fastened with hooks and laces at the front, and hinged at the back. This meant a soldier was well protected, but the armor was flexible enough that the soldier could move and bend. A soldier also wore a metal helmet that extended at the back guard to protect the neck from sword blows. Some had pieces that covered the cheeks and nose, too. Underneath the armor, a Roman soldier wore a linen shirt, a woolen tunic, and a woolen or linen scarf, called a focale. The focale protected the soldier's neck from being rubbed sore by the heavy armor.

# Fighting Battles

There were around 500,000 soldiers in the Roman army when it was at its largest. To keep large numbers of men in order, the army was divided into 30 large groups, called legions.

## Roman Legions

Each legion in the Roman army had up to 6,000 soldiers, who were called legionaries. Officers in charge of a legion were called legates. Each legion had a long pole with a flag or badge for identification. Each legion was further divided into ten cohorts, or units. Each cohort contained six groups or troops of about 80 legionaries, called centuries. The centurion was the soldier in charge of a century. The short rod he carried at all times showed his rank, and could be used to hit soldiers who disobeyed orders.

### THE MIGHT OF THE LEGION

**Each legion also carried an aquila—an image of an eagle perched on top of a pole. The eagle represented the strength of the legion. Legions fought to the death to take back an aquila stolen in battle.**

## Fearless Forces

Most Roman soldiers were infantry, walking and fighting on foot. Some were part of a cavalry and rode horses. Battle signals were given by trumpet, which soldiers followed immediately. Roman soldiers were highly organized and attacked in tight formations. Often, the cavalry were lined up on both sides of the infantry. They shot a burst of weapons, then marched steadily toward the enemy, using their strong shields for protection. If attacked by arrows and rocks from above, a signal was given to form a testudo, or tortoise. Soldiers quickly interlocked their shields in a neat and tight formation to surround and protect themselves, like a tortoise shell. They could then continue moving forward safely. At the last minute, they hurled spears, and charged at the enemy with their swords and other hand weapons. The cavalry chased any enemies who tried to flee.

### ANALYZE THE ANCIENTS

This is a modern reenactment of Roman soldiers in a battle formation. Using the information you have learned so far, can you answer these questions?

1. This is the testudo, or tortoise, formation. How do you think it got this name and how did it keep even one soldier from getting hurt?

2. For this formation to work, all the soldiers in the group had to act quickly and position their shields accurately. What does this tell us about the Roman army?

# CHAPTER 3

# Roman Beliefs

The Romans worshiped many gods and goddesses. They also took on some new gods from people they conquered, such as the goddess Isis from Egypt, and adopted and renamed many Greek gods.

## Famous Gods and Goddesses

Jupiter was king of the gods and he killed enemies using lightning bolts and thunder. His queen was Juno, goddess of women and marriage. Neptune was the god of the sea. He carried a three-pronged trident and rode a dolphin or horse. Mars was the god of war and the father of Romulus and Remus. March is named after Mars because it was the month soldiers began fighting after winter. Pluto was the god of the dead and ruler of the **underworld**. Saturn was the god of time, and his weapon was a **scythe**.

### GOD OF THE SEA

**This beautiful mosaic of Neptune shows the god holding a trident in his right hand, alongside the two sea horses that Roman legend says pulled his chariot.**

# The Underworld

The ancient Romans believed that when a person died, they traveled across the River of the Dead, called the Styx, to the underworld. They buried bodies with a coin in their mouth to pay the ferryman, Charon, to take them across the river. The dead then had to get past Cerberus, a vicious three-headed dog, which let only the dead meet the judges of the dead. The judges sent warriors and heroes to the Fields of Elysium. Ordinary people went to the Plain of Asphodel. Criminals went to a hell called Tartarus to be tortured as punishment for the bad things they had done. As well as a coin for the ferryman, Romans buried their dead with other objects for the afterlife (life after death), such as food, makeup, and jewelry.

## ANALYZE THE ANCIENTS

This is a sculpture of the god Jupiter. Based on the information you have learned, can you answer these questions to analyze the Romans?

1. Why do you think Jupiter is shown in this sculpture as holding a scepter—the long stick that symbolizes royalty?

2. The eagle rules the skies, flying high to see over the greatest area and is a hunter of other birds. Why do you think Romans saw this bird as Jupiter's sacred animal?

# Towering Temples

The Romans built many temples where they could worship their gods. Temples were large, ornate, and usually built in important positions, such as at one side of a city's forum, or alongside a main road or avenue.

## Many Temples

There were many Roman temples because each one was dedicated to a particular god or goddess, or sometimes several. Roman generals mainly built temples dedicated to Mars to thank him for their victories in battle. If someone wanted to pray to find a husband or wife, they would go to a temple dedicated to Venus—the goddess of love. Some temples were even dedicated to the emperors who had been proclaimed as part-gods.

Roman temples were very important places. They usually stood on a high platform called a podium, which was reached by climbing a long, steep flight of steps. This made the temples stand out and emphasized their importance. The steps were faced, or covered, in a fine white plaster, called stucco, or high-quality marble stone. They were often decorated with marble sculptures or **reliefs**. To lift heavy stones and slabs, the Romans used cranes. **Slaves** or animals turned a treadmill or pulled on ropes to power the cranes.

### GODDESS OF GOOD HEALTH

**People often brought offerings to temple statues like this one of Hygeia, the ancient goddess of good health.**

IMPORTANT TEMPLES

**Temples were built on a platform so they stood high up to emphasize their importance.**

## Inside the Temples

Inside a temple, there was a main room called a cella. The cella contained a bronze or stone image or sculpture of the god the to whom the temple was dedicated. There was also a small **altar** where people prayed to or worshiped the god. In small rooms in the temple, attendants stored equipment and offerings. The front entrance was always grand with a deep, wide porch, called a portico. The portico usually had a row of columns with a wide, open area behind it, in front of the cella. The walls were often covered in frescoes (paintings made on plaster) depicting gods or everyday life. Treasures were sometimes kept in underground chambers below the temples.

# Ceremonies and Rituals

In Rome, people believed that they had to keep the gods and goddesses happy to receive good luck. They had to worship their gods and make offerings at temples and shrines every day, and during special **rituals** or celebrations. The rituals had to be followed carefully to make them work.

## Prayers and Offerings

The Romans had a huge number of prayers they could use, and there were specific prayers for almost anything. There were prayers to bring bad luck on an enemy, and for getting back stolen goods, for example. When people said a prayer, they usually made a small offering to the god at the same time. These offerings could take the form of foods such as milk, fruit, cheese, or wine. However, people often offered up an animal **sacrifice**, as a symbol of life. For large official ceremonies when a whole community gathered in worship at a temple, there were almost always animal sacrifices.

ANCIENT AMPHORA

**This large jug, called an amphora, was used to hold offerings of wine, milk, and honey for temple worship.**

## Sacrifices

A person or family could make an animal sacrifice at home, on an altar in a hall, or at a temple. Traders outside the Roman temples sold small birds and animals for people to buy and give as offerings. Public ceremonies usually took place in an open space in front of the temple close to the altar. All ceremonies had to be carried out on a certain date and in a certain way. Specific objects surrounded the image of the god, and the same actions were performed each time. Different animals were sacrificed for different gods. Priests sacrificed one ram for Janus, the god of new beginnings, a young cow or heifer for Jupiter, and an ox, a pig, and a sheep for Mars. Each year on October 15, after a chariot race, one of the winning horses would be sacrificed to Mars.

SACRIFICING A BULL

**This carving illustrates the ceremonial sacrifice of a bull.**

CHAPTER 4

# Work and Trade

As cities and settlements in the Roman world grew and prospered, there were many different kinds of jobs to do. But the majority of people still lived in the countryside and worked on the land. Roman farms were important for feeding a growing population. Being a farmer was seen as a worthwhile profession.

## Rich and Poor

Early Roman farmers had small plots of land where they grew just enough wheat, barley, beans, vegetables, and fruit to feed their families. Some rich farmers had a house in the city and a grand house, called a villa, on a country farm. They had slaves who they forced to do all the farm work. Even ordinary farmers often had one slave or more. Farmers and slaves used iron or wooden tools such as hoes, rakes, and spades. They used **sickles** to harvest grains and other crops, and developed a form of plow to turn over the soil for planting. They raised chickens, pigs, sheep, and goats for milk, eggs, and meat. They also kept bees for honey.

ROMAN MILLSTONE

**This millstone, used for crushing olives to extract their oil, was found in the ancient Roman city of Volubilis in Morocco.**

## OLIVES FOR OIL

The Romans used olive oil for cooking, to make perfume, and to treat illnesses. They also used it in religious rituals, and burned it for light inside homes and temples. Olive oil was transported around the empire and stored in containers called amphorae, like these.

# Crops of the Empire

The three most important products grown and traded by farmers in the Roman world were grains, grapes for wine, and olives used to make olive oil. Italian farms produced large amounts of food, but crops grown in different areas were also transported around the empire. Growing grains, such as wheat, was very important. A lot of wheat that was used to make the bread that fed the large Roman army was grown in England and in Egypt. It was then shipped to cities such as Rome. The Romans took olive plants to all their **colonies** so the farmers could learn to grow them. Olives were grown in Spain, Italy, and North Africa, then **imported** to Rome. Grapes were grown in Rome to make into wine. The wine was then **exported** to the provinces, often in exchange for slaves.

# Jobs for All

As the Roman Empire grew, the variety of jobs available in Rome also increased. There were bakers, merchants, tradesmen such as blacksmiths, and craftspeople such as jewelers and sculptors. The more highly educated people worked as doctors, engineers, lawyers, and government officials.

## Artists and Craftspeople

Craftspeople were very important to the empire. As well as making useful items such as pots and weapons, they also made decorative objects and jewelry. Some craftspeople learned their trade from their parents and worked in small, family businesses. Other workshops were huge, with many slaves producing large numbers of objects, rather like factories today. Goldsmiths made jewelry and decorative items. Leather workers made purses, pouches, sandals, clothing, and shields. Sculptors made statues out of stone. Musicians were employed for religious ceremonies and to entertain people. Mosaic workers created intricate floors and walls for houses and temples. These beautiful artworks were made from more than a million tiny pieces of colored stone.

MOSAIC FLOOR

**Mosaics were very expensive to produce. Only the very wealthy could afford mosaics in their homes. This mosaic of musicians was uncovered in the ruins of Pompeii.**

TEACHING YOUNG BOYS

One of the most important jobs of teachers was to teach Roman boys public speaking skills. These skills helped the boys become successful politicians and lawyers when they grew up.

## Educated Professionals

The Romans created a set of written laws and had lawyers and judges to make sure the laws were upheld fairly. The government of Rome was huge. There were all sorts of government jobs, from tax collectors to record keepers. Engineering was another highly skilled job. Engineers designed and built lighthouses, bridges, roads, temples, and palaces, many of which still exist today. Doctors in Rome were often educated Greeks, who were brought to Rome as slaves. The doctors developed hospitals to treat wounded soldiers at army camps. The Romans also trained nurses, who then worked in the battlefields. The early Romans had taught their own children. But later, the Romans who could afford it employed teachers to educate their children. They adopted this idea from the Greeks, and teachers were often educated Greek slaves.

# Merchants and Trade

Trade was vital to Rome. It was very expensive running an empire and keeping a large, well-trained army. Trade brought in much of the money that was needed.

## Trade Routes

The Romans developed many trade routes along which they exported and imported goods. Their ships sailed from the port of Ostia to and from lands around the Mediterranean Sea and beyond. Goods were brought on barges up the Tiber River to the city. Roman roads allowed merchants to travel easily. One of the oldest and busiest roads was the Via Salaria, the salt route, along which Roman merchants brought carts full of salt. Roman merchants imported a variety of goods including beef, corn, glass, iron, lead, leather, marble, olive oil, perfume, dye, silk, silver, spices, wood, tin, and wine from as far away as China and Africa.

EXPORT AND IMPORT

**This ancient mosaic shows an elephant from Africa being loaded onto a ship bound for Rome.**

## Currency and Counting

Trade was so important to the Romans that they introduced a system of money that was used all over their empire. This made it easy for merchants to trade anywhere, using the same coins, whether in Britain, Africa, or Rome. It meant that they did not need to figure out what one set of coins might be worth in another country's currency (money) whenever they made a deal. There were three types of Roman coins: gold (aureus), silver (denarius), and brass (sestertius, dupondius, and as). Two asses were worth 1 dupondius, 2 dupondii were worth 1 sestertius, 4 sestertic were worth 1 denarius, and 25 denarii were worth 1 aureus. Some coins had pictures of emperors on them to help make an emperor more famous. The Romans also produced a lightweight abacus—a counting device that merchants, engineers, and tax collectors could carry with them to make calculations.

### ANALYZE THE ANCIENTS

These are the Roman coins. Can you use the information you have learned to answer these questions to analyze the Romans?

1. How did using the same coins throughout the empire help the Romans trade more easily?

2. Why did the coins have images of Roman emperors on them? How could this have helped to spread an emperor's fame?

# CHAPTER 5

# Roman Innovations

The Romans were always on the lookout for good ideas. They borrowed many inventions and technologies from the people they conquered or they came into contact with when trading. Romans did invent some new things themselves. However, they were especially skilled at making changes to other people's technology to make it even better.

## Arches and Aqueducts

Although they did not invent the arch, the Romans were the first people to include arches in their huge bridges and aqueducts. An aqueduct was like a bridge, built on arches, with a stone channel on top to carry water. The aqueduct sloped downhill toward a town. It supplied the townpeople with water, especially during summer, when it could be very hot and dry. When the population of Rome reached its peak of 1 million inhabitants, the aqueducts provided up to 200 gallons (757 l) of water for every person every day. The water flowed from higher ground through the aqueducts into giant storage pools, called cisterns. Water was carried from these cisterns and around the city through lead pipes.

PONT DU GARD

**Some Roman aqueducts were so well made that they still stand today—2,000 years later! This Roman aqueduct is Pont du Gard in the south of France.**

THE PANTHEON

**The Pantheon in Rome, with its beautiful dome, was built 18 centuries ago. It is a fine example of a Roman building made from long-lasting concrete.**

## The First Concrete

One reason that aqueducts and so many other Roman structures are still standing today is because they were built from a very strong, long-lasting type of concrete. The Roman recipe for concrete was a mix of ash from volcanoes, a mineral called lime, seawater, and volcanic rocks. This concrete was so strong and waterproof that it was used not only to build aqueducts, but also to line **reservoirs** that stored vast amounts of water. It was also used to hold together piers, harbors, and breakwaters (walls to hold back waves). Roman concrete has survived 2,000 years of being beaten by ocean waves. This is because the seawater in the concrete reacts with the volcanic material and creates new minerals that make the concrete even stronger.

# Public Health

The Roman aqueducts provided the Romans with freshwater for keeping clean. The water was also used for sewer systems that carried dirty water away from the city. Fresh, clean water and sewers are important for public health. Without them, there is risk that people will catch diseases from drinking dirty water or from filthy sewage left around streets and homes.

## Sewers and Drains

Rome and other major cities had a network of covered sewers and drains. Most of the buildings in the city were connected to them. Rome had laundries where workers washed people's clothes. The city also had public toilets, some of which had enough seats for up to 60 people. There were seven sewers, one of which was big enough to drive a wagon through. Water from local streams was regularly used to flush the drains and sewers. Drains carried the wastewater away from the city and dumped it into the Tiber River. In Rome, 300 slaves cleaned the streets and the public toilets at night while the Romans were asleep.

### ROMAN TOILETS

**Roman toilets were sometimes flushed using water from bathhouses. Romans did not have toilet paper, so they often used a sponge on a stick to clean themselves.**

ROMAN BATHHOUSES

**Romans in England could go to the magnificent bathhouses in the city of Bath. There, they could get clean, swim in the waters, and pray to the goddess Minerva. The Romans believed Minerva had healing powers.**

## Bathhouses

As well as supplying buildings and fountains with water, the aqueducts also brought water to the Roman bathhouses. Bathhouses were public baths in which Romans washed themselves. Most bathhouses charged very small entrance fees. Rome had nine public baths. There were three types of baths: people could go from the very hot "caldarium" to the warm "tepidarium," then the cold "frigidarium." Water was heated by hot air from a furnace that was carried around the bathhouse through clay or tile pipes. The hot air was used to heat the floors and the water in the baths above. Many baths had exercise rooms attached to them. Baths were so important that some government officials had the job of checking to make sure they were all clean.

# Roman Systems

The Romans also invented systems of naming dates and numbers to be used across the empire. This system made sure that all Romans were on the same schedule.

## The Julian Calendar

When Julius Caesar was in a position of power, he invented a new calendar called the Julian calendar. It had 12 months with 365 days each year for three years, and 366 days on the fourth year, just like the calendar we use today. Julius Caesar named the month of July after himself. When Augustus Caesar became emperor, he named the next month "August" after himself. However, August had only 30 days, not 31 like July. So, to fix that, the Romans took a day from February and added it to August. That is why today, February is the shortest month of the year.

## Roman Numerals

Roman numerals were developed so that the Romans could easily price different goods and services across the empire. Roman numerals are represented by seven different letters: I, V, X, L, C, D, and M. These letters represent the numbers 1, 5, 10, 50, 100, 500, and 1,000. The letters can be combined to make different numbers. For example, the Roman numeral for two is written as II. The numeral 12 is written as XII (ten plus two), the number 28 is written as XXVIII.

### EASY TRADING

**Roman merchants traveling afar found it easier to trade with others in the empire when they all used the same counting system.**

## Roman Newspapers

The Romans are also credited with inventing one of the world's first newspapers—the *Acta Diurna*, or Daily Events. These papers were first published on the orders of Julius Caesar. He wanted to tell people about important official announcements. The news updates were carved in stone or sometimes on metal. They were then displayed in important public places, such as the baths. That way, people from all over Rome could see the news.

### ANALYZE THE ANCIENTS

This is an inscription on a statue of the Roman emperor, Marcus Aurelius. Using your knowledge of Roman numerals, can you answer these questions?

1. On this inscription are the numbers XXVII, VI, and III. What do these numbers mean?

2. How did the system of Roman numerals help the Romans build their empire?

# CHAPTER 6

# Everyday Life

The kind of everyday life a person led in Rome depended on their wealth and status. The homes that people lived in are one example of the big differences in the lives of rich and poor Romans.

## Homes for the Rich

Rich Romans lived in beautiful homes in the town. Their homes were on one floor and built around a central courtyard that was open to the sky. The courtyard often had a garden. Off the courtyard, there were many rooms. There was a kitchen, bathroom, dining room, bedrooms, and rooms for the slaves who had to serve the rich Romans. Along the front of the home was a long, covered porch that helped keep the rooms cool in the summer. Rich Romans had central heating, which they used in winter. Slaves kept furnaces burning all winter. Furnaces fed warm air through spaces under the floors and between the walls to keep the building cozy. Some rich Romans also had villas in the countryside with pools and large gardens.

CENTRAL COURTYARDS

**Wealthy Roman homes were usually set around an open courtyard like this.**

FABULOUS FRESCOES

The walls in a wealthy family's home were often covered in rich, colorful paintings called frescoes.

## Apartment Blocks and Huts

The poorer people in Rome often lived in flats in a kind of apartment block. Some of these buildings took up a whole block in the capital city. The apartment buildings were between three to seven floors tall. Flats usually had only one or two rooms and no running water. The ground-floor rooms were made of brick or stone and were often used by businesses or shops. These businesses might have sold food to the tenants (people who rent a property) of the flats above them, who found it too risky to cook in the wooden rooms. Farmhouses were small huts with one or two rooms. Farm animals were often kept in the huts with the farmers to keep them safe, and to keep them warm in winter. Furniture in both rich and poor houses was fairly simple. People sat on wooden benches or couches. Beds were wooden frames with leather straps strung across the frame.

# Food and Fashion

In the Roman world, even the food you ate and the clothes you wore told people how wealthy and important you were.

## Roman Food

Ordinary Romans ate simple meals mainly of beans and a kind of porridge made from wheat, millet, and corn, called pottage. They also ate a lot of bread and vegetables. Roman food was flavored with salt, pepper, and other spices. Romans also drank wine, usually with a lot of water in it. Rich people added meat or wine to their pottage. They also enjoyed a pudding made from bread soaked in milk, then fried in butter and covered with honey. They often invited guests to feasts of foods from all over the empire to show off their wealth. They ordered extravagant dishes such as peacock brains or flamingo tongues. Another dish was a hare (rabbit) that was roasted with bird's wings attached to it so it looked like a flying horse.

ROMAN BANQUET

**This painting found in the ruins of Pompeii shows a Roman banquet.**

## Roman Clothes

Roman men wore a knee-length tunic. It had a cloak like a wide shawl that draped over one shoulder and wrapped around the body. Important Roman men wore a long robe called a toga. Women wore an ankle-length tunic. It had a long, pleated dress called a stola over it, which had clasps at the shoulders. Rich women had slaves to help them dress, put on jewelry, makeup, and perfume. They also made fancy hairstyles. Children wore similar tunics to the adults. The color of a person's clothes told a lot about them. Only emperors were allowed to wear purple togas. Purple dye was made from a lot of small, tropical sea snails. The dye cost three times the yearly wage of a Roman baker. Emperors wore purple to show their importance.

### ANALYZE THE ANCIENTS

This is a mosaic of a Roman emperor. Using the information you have read, can you answer these questions to analyze the Romans?

1. How can you tell this is an emperor from the clothes he is wearing? Hint: the purple of his tunic has faded over time!

2. Why was purple the color of the emperors?

# Family Life

Although the lives of rich and poor were different in many ways, there were some similarities. Family was very important to all Romans, and a whole family usually lived together. When a daughter married, she went to live with her husband's family.

## Fathers and Mothers

In any Roman family, the oldest male, called the paterfamilias, was head of the household. The paterfamilias held all the power. Only he could own property. He also decided what jobs his children and grandchildren would do, and whom they would marry. Even after they were married, sons and grandsons received an allowance from the family business. This continued until the paterfamilias died, and the sons and grandsons could take over the business. The rest of the family had to do what the paterfamilias said, as long as he was fair. If they disobeyed, he was allowed by law to sell his children into slavery. Women were expected to run the home, cook meals, and raise children. However, during the time of the Roman Empire, women could also own and **inherit** property, and have a paid job.

ROMAN MARRIAGE

**This carving shows a couple getting married. The bride's belt may show the knot symbolizing that the husband was "belted and bound" to her.**

BEWARE OF THE DOG!

**This Roman mosaic of a family dog includes the phrase "cave canem" meaning "beware of the dog!"**

## Children in Rome

The paterfamilias taught boys in the family a trade, and to read and write. They also taught them other skills, such as how to behave around other people. Mothers taught their daughters how to cook, make clothes, and take care of the home. Many girls were married by the age of 14 to someone their family had chosen. Roman children played with toys similar to the toys children play with today. They had toy soldiers, rattles, balls, doll houses, carts, and pull-along animals on wheels. They also had scooters, yo-yos, marbles, and skipping ropes. Some Roman children had pets, too, such as dogs, pigeons and other birds, or monkeys. Poor children often had to spend more time working with their families. When they had free time, they played with wooden dolls and played games using pebbles for counters.

# Games and Races

The lives of the poor were hard, and they relaxed by watching the popular entertainment of Roman times: chariot races or **gladiators** fighting to their deaths.

## Gladiators

Gladiator events happened in vast outdoor theaters called amphitheaters. To gain favor with their people, emperors often paid for these events. This meant that ordinary people could watch for free. Sometimes, there were even free snacks served. Spectators watched brutal fights between different gladiators, or gladiators and wild animals, such as lions brought from Africa. These events were horribly bloody. In some, up to 10,000 animals could be killed in a single day. Most gladiators were criminals, prisoners of war, or slaves bought for the event. When a gladiator was beaten but still alive, the audience decided whether he should live or die. They tucked their thumbs into their closed fists if they liked him so he could live. But if they wanted him killed, they waved scarves or put their thumbs out.

In one of the most famous amphitheaters, the Colosseum, there were tunnels under the floor where the animals and gladiators were kept. There were also trapdoors in the arena for special effects. Large amphitheaters like this were sometimes flooded with water so that there could be water shows with real boats and crocodiles.

FAMOUS AMPHITHEATER

**The Colosseum in Rome had 80 entrances and could seat 50,000 spectators. It is as tall as a 12-story building.**

### CHARIOT RACES

**There were four teams of chariot racers. Each one wore different team colors. People supported different teams of chariot racers the way people support different sports teams today.**

## Chariot Races

Chariot races were held in a huge, oval stadium in Rome named the Circus Maximus. Chariot racing was a dangerous sport in which drivers could be killed. Chariots were small, two-wheeled carts, driven by one man and pulled by four horses. The chariots raced seven laps around the stadium watched by up to 200,000 spectators. Chariots were light, so they could move quickly. But that meant they also toppled over easily when the chariots crashed into each other in the heat of the race. If drivers fell out, they were often trampled by the speeding horses pulling other chariots.

# The End of the Empire

The beginning of the end for the Roman Empire came when it was divided into two. It had one capital city and ruler in Rome, and another in Byzantium—an ancient city on the site of present-day Istanbul in Turkey. This began to weaken the empire and left it open to attack from invaders. Those invaders removed the last Roman emperors from power.

## The Romans and Christianity

Byzantium was established and ruled by Emperor Constantine. He named his new city Constantinople, after himself. Before Constantine, Christians were often arrested and even put to death. One possible reason is because they refused to make sacrifices to the Roman gods and emperors. Then Emperor Constantine turned away from the Roman religion. He became a Christian, and everything changed. He made Christianity the official religion of the Roman Empire in the fourth century AD. This brought an end to the Roman religion that had played a part in uniting the different peoples of the empire for so long. As Roman emperors became weaker, Christian leaders became more powerful.

### PRINCE ODOACER

**Many historians consider the end of the Roman Empire to have been the moment when Prince Odoacer took control of Rome and made himself king of Italy.**

## Under Attack

By the fifth century AD, the Roman Empire was falling apart. There was a series of weak emperors and **civil wars** in parts of the empire. Respect for Roman law was fading. Rome was also under attack from the tribes of Goths, Huns, and Vandals from northern Europe. Romans called these enemies "barbarians" because they thought they were uncivilized. These invaders destroyed many of the great buildings of Rome and killed many of its people. In AD 476, a German prince named Odoacer forced the last Roman Emperor, Romulus Augustus, to step down. Odoacer took control of Rome and made himself king of Italy. The eastern part of the Roman Empire survived until AD 453, when the **Ottoman Turks** took it over.

### EVIDENCE OF THE ROMAN EMPIRE

**The Roman Empire ended long ago, but the evidence of it is all around us. This is the outside of the mighty Colosseum in Rome today.**

# Answers

Did you manage to analyze the ancients? Check your answers against the correct answers on these pages.

## PAGE 9

1. The tablets and scroll tells us that the Romans valued education. If people were educated, they wanted to show off that fact in paintings they had painted of themselves.
2. The position of the baker's wife in the painting suggests she is a working woman and his equal in their business.

## PAGE 15

1. The testudo formation got its name because soldiers fit their shields all around them, so they looked like a tortoise with a shell completely covering its body. They interlocked the shields so that no missiles could get through, so no one would be hurt.
2. The Roman army was well trained and obeyed orders immediately. They reacted quickly and knew exactly where to position their shields accurately. This tells us the Roman army was very organized and well controlled, and that the shields the soldiers had were very strong.

## PAGE 17

1. Jupiter is holding a scepter to show that he is king of the gods and rules over the other gods.
2. Jupiter's sacred animal is an eagle because these birds rule the skies just as Jupiter rules the heavens.

## PAGE 27

1. Using the same coins throughout the empire helped Roman merchants buy and sell things easily because they did not have to figure out what one set of coins might be worth in another country's currency whenever they made a deal.
2. Roman coins were used all over the empire, far from Rome where the emperor lived. So the coins helped to spread the emperor's image and fame all over the empire.

# Answers

PAGE 33

1. Number XXVII is 27, VI is 6, and III is 3.
2. The system of Roman numerals was developed so that the Romans could easily price different goods and services across the empire.

PAGE 37

1. Only emperors were allowed to wear purple togas.
2. Purple was the color of the emperors because it was incredibly expensive to produce, so it showed how important the emperor was.

# Glossary

**altar** table or platform where religious rituals are carried out

**artifacts** objects from the past that tell us about people's lives in history

**battering rams** heavy beams used to break down gates

**civil wars** wars between two or more parts of the same country

**close combat** fighting opponents at short range

**colonies** countries or regions controlled by a different country that is often far away

**culture** the beliefs, customs, and arts of a particular group of people or country

**customs** traditional actions or ways of behaving that are common to people in a particular group or place

**emperor** male ruler or king

**empire** large area of land or group of countries ruled over by one leader

**exported** took to another country to sell

**gladiators** men trained to fight

**heir** person who inherits a title

**imported** bought and brought in from another country

**inherit** get from one's parents

**legend** story from ancient times that is not always true

**merchants** people who buy and sell goods

**offerings** things that people give as part of a religious ceremony or ritual

**Ottoman Turks** people from the Ottoman Empire, ruled by Turkish tribes in the 1400s and 1500s

**provinces** regions or territories ruled or governed as part of an empire

**reliefs** sculptures in which shapes and figures are raised up above the surface of the stone

**republic** state in which the citizens vote for a group of people to govern them

**reservoirs** artificial lakes for collecting and storing freshwater

**rituals** religious ceremonies

**sacrifice** something killed to honor a god or gods

**scythe** tool with a long, curved blade at the end of a long pole

**sickles** hand tools with a curved blade used for cutting grains

**slaves** people who are owned by other people and have to obey them

**temples** buildings where people go to worship their god or gods

**underworld** mythical world of the dead

# For More Information

## Books

Croy, Anita. *How Did Rome Rise and Fall?*. New York, NY: Cavendish Square Publishing, 2017.

Deem, James M. *Bodies from the Ash: Life and Death in Ancient Pompeii.* Boston, MA: HMH Books for Young Readers, 2017.

Randolph, Joanne. *Living and Working in Ancient Rome*. New York, NY: Enslow Publishing, 2017.

Stokes, Jonathan W. *The Thrifty Guide to Ancient Rome: A Handbook for Time Travelers.* New York, NY: Viking Books, 2018.

Waxman, Laura Hamilton. *Mysteries of Pompeii.* Minneapolis, MN: Lerner Publications, 2017.

## Websites

There's a wealth of information about ancient Rome at:
**www.ancient.eu/Rome**

Find out more about the history of Rome at:
**www.history.com/topics/ancient-history/ancient-rome**

Follow a timeline of ancient Rome at:
**www.timemaps.com/civilizations/ancient-rome**

Publisher's note to educators and parents: Our editors have carefully reviewed these websites to ensure that they are suitable for students. Many websites change frequently, however, and we cannot guarantee that a site's future contents will continue to meet our high standards of quality and educational value. Be advised that students should be closely supervised whenever they access the Internet.

# Index